KN   APR '93

FLIT, FLUTTER, FLY!

A Doubleday Book for Young Readers

FLIT,

Illustrated by Peter Palagonia

Poems about bugs and other crawly creatures

FLUTTER, FLY!

SELECTED BY Lee Bennett Hopkins

To
Diane Arico
BEE-cause...

LBH

For
my nephew Ben

PP

A Doubleday Book for Young Readers
PUBLISHED BY Delacorte Press
Bantam Doubleday Dell Publishing Group, Inc.
666 Fifth Avenue, New York, New York 10103

DOUBLEDAY and the portrayal of an anchor with a dolphin
are trademarks of Bantam Doubleday Dell Publishing Group, Inc.
Copyright © 1992 by Lee Bennett Hopkins
Illustrations copyright © 1992 by Peter Palagonia

Library of Congress Cataloging in Publication Data
Flit, flutter, fly!: poems about bugs and other crawly creatures /
selected by Lee Bennett Hopkins; illustrated by Peter Palagonia. — 1st ed.
        p.   cm.
Summary: A collection of poems by a variety of authors about bugs and other creatures that crawl.
ISBN 0-385-41468-4.
1. Insects—Juvenile poetry. 2. Children's poetry, American. 3. Children's poetry, English. [1. Insects—Poetry.
2. American poetry—Collections. 3. English poetry—Collections.] I. Hopkins, Lee Bennett. II. Palagonia, Peter,
ill.
PS595.I56F45   1992   811'.508036—dc20   91-12441   CIP   AC

Manufactured in U.S.A.
November 1992

10   9   8   7   6   5   4   3   2   1

Contents

Acknowledgments

Curtis Brown, Ltd., for "How?" and "Ladybug" by Lee Bennett Hopkins. Copyright © 1992 by Lee Bennett Hopkins. Used by permission of Curtis Brown, Ltd./Lillian M. Fisher for "Lady Spider" and "A Magic House." Used by permission of the author, who controls all rights./Isabel Joshlin Glaser for "Fishing." Used by permission of the author, who controls all rights./Alfred A. Knopf, Inc., for "Snail" from *Selected Poems of Langston Hughes.* Copyright 1947 by Langston Hughes. By permission of Alfred A. Knopf, Inc./HarperCollins Publishers, for "Bugs" from *Dogs & Dragons Tree & Dreams* by Karla Kuskin, which originally appeared in *Alexander Soames: His Poems* by Karla Kuskin. Copyright © 1962 by Karla Kuskin; "Bumblebee" from *Out in the Dark and Daylight* by Aileen Fisher. Copyright © 1980 by Aileen Fisher. Reprinted by permission of HarperCollins Publishers./J. Patrick Lewis for "Fireflies." Used by permission of the author, who controls all rights./Sandra Liatsos for "A Picnic." Used by permission of the author, who controls all rights./Little, Brown & Company for "Glow-worm" from *One at a Time* by David McCord. Copyright © 1966, 1962 by David McCord. By permission of Little, Brown & Company./Beverly McLoughland for "Buggy Love." Used by permission of the author, who controls all rights./Macmillan Publishing Company for "Snails" from *Remembering and Other Poems* by Myra Cohn Livingston. Copyright © 1989 by Myra Cohn Livingston. Reprinted with permission of Margaret K. McElderry Books, an imprint of Macmillan Publishing Company./G.P. Putnam's Sons for "Inch-Worm" from *Hello Day* by Dorothy Aldis. Copyright 1959 by Dorothy Aldis, copyright © renewed 1989 by Roy E. Porter. Reprinted by permission of G. P. Putnam's Sons./Marian Reiner for "Crickets" from *Crickets and Bullfrogs and Whispers of Thunder* by Harry Behn. Copyright © 1949, 1953, 1956, 1957, 1966, 1968 by Harry Behn. Copyright renewed; "Hey, Bug!" from *I Feel the Same Way* by Lilian Moore. Copyright © 1967 by Lilian Moore. Both reprinted by permission of Marian Reiner for the authors./The Shoe String Press, Inc., for "Bugs" from *The Fish with a Deep Sea Smile* by Margaret Wise Brown (Linnet Books: Hamden, Connecticut, 1988) by permission of the publisher.

Bugs

I am very fond of bugs.
I kiss them
And I give them hugs.

KARLA KUSKIN

A Wish

I wish I was a little grub
With whiskers round my tummy.
I'd climb into a honeypot
And make my tummy gummy,
And then I'd crawl all over you
And make your tummy gummy too.

ANONYMOUS

Glowworm

Never talk down to a glowworm—
Such as *What do you knowworm?*
How's it down belowworm?
Guess you're quite a slowworm.
No. Just say
                    Hellowworm!

DAVID MCCORD

Crickets

We cannot say that crickets sing
Since all they do is twang a wing.

Especially when the wind is still
They orchestrate a sunlit hill,

And in the evening blue above
They weave the stars and moon with love,

Then peacefully they chirp all night
Remembering delight, delight…

HARRY BEHN

Lady Spider

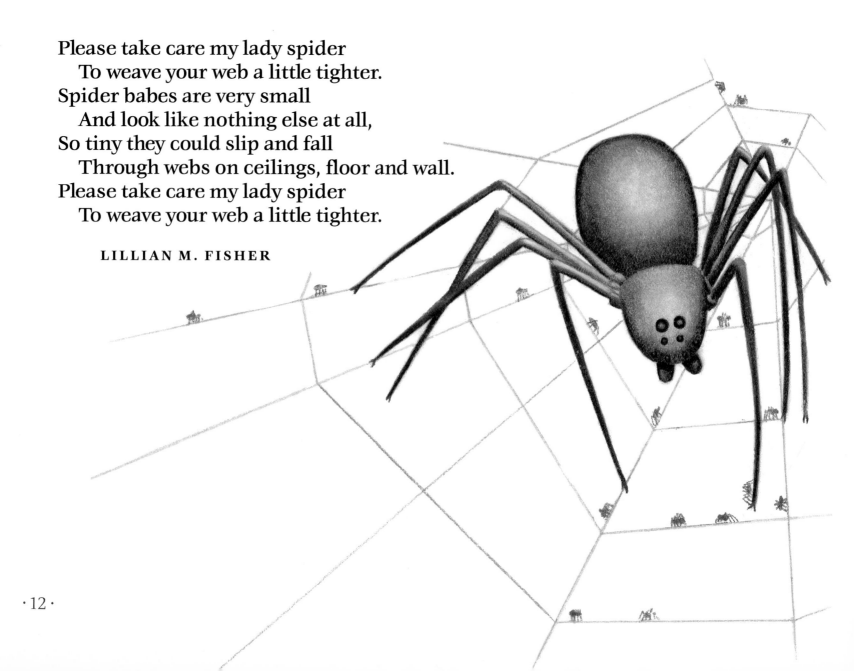

Please take care my lady spider
   To weave your web a little tighter.
Spider babes are very small
   And look like nothing else at all,
So tiny they could slip and fall
   Through webs on ceilings, floor and wall.
Please take care my lady spider
   To weave your web a little tighter.

LILLIAN M. FISHER

A Picnic

We had a picnic
by the lake.
We ate
some sandwiches
and cake.

We munched
and crunched
till we were through.

We liked the taste.
The ants did, too.

SANDRA LIATSOS

Snails

Clinging to our stucco wall,
holding tight,
they never fall.

Resting on a zinnia stem,
they nibble leaves.
I look at them,

tracing their path
of sticky slime,
wondering where I would climb

if I could ooze a shining trail,
if I could travel
like a snail.

MYRA COHN LIVINGSTON

Snail

Little snail,
Dreaming you go.
Weather and rose
Is all you know.

Weather and rose
Is all you see,
Drinking
The dewdrop's
Mystery.

LANGSTON HUGHES

Fishing

A dragonfly darts over the pond,
    Flashes sudden blue
    As if slices
    Of sky fell
Through the quick nets
    Of its wings…

Nothing else. Nothing.
Just me on the banks,
    And that dragonfly
Whirly-bugging in the sun.
    So quiet, I hear
    How silence sings.

ISABEL JOSHLIN GLASER

Caterpillar

Brown and furry
Caterpillar in a hurry;
Take your walk
To the shady leaf or stalk.

May no toad spy you,
May the little birds pass by you;
Spin and die,
To live again a butterfly.

CHRISTINA G. ROSSETTI

A Magic House

Someone's little silken house
   is hanging by a thread.
A brown cocoon looks like a leaf
   as shown in books I've read.
It swings among the poplar leaves,
   I watch it and I giggle,
Because whatever is inside
   makes me wiggle-waggle-wiggle.

The little home has burst its skin
   and someone's coming out,
Now slowly getting bigger
   as it twists and turns about.
My heart begins to flutter,
   though I dare not move a hair.
Suddenly…like magic…
   a *butterfly*…is *there*!

LILLIAN M. FISHER

How?

How
do
spiders,
ants,
ladybugs,
bees—

butterflies,
fireflies,
dragonflies,
fleas—

know

to
crawl,
creep,
flit,
flutter,
fly—

as
winter
comes
bitterly
chilling
the
sky?

LEE BENNETT HOPKINS

· 21 ·

Fireflies

An August night—
  The wind not quite
A wind, the sky
  Not just a sky—
And everywhere
  The speckled air
Of summer stars
  Alive in jars.

J. PATRICK LEWIS

Buggy Love

The light that
Fireflies
Create
Is meant to woo
A loving mate—
Will you?
Won't you?
Yes and no,
On and off
And touch and
Go—
Buggy love wins
With hugs and kisses,
Congratulations!
Mr.
Mrs.

BEVERLY MCLOUGHLAND

Butterfly

What is a butterfly?
At best
He's but a caterpillar
Dressed.

BENJAMIN FRANKLIN

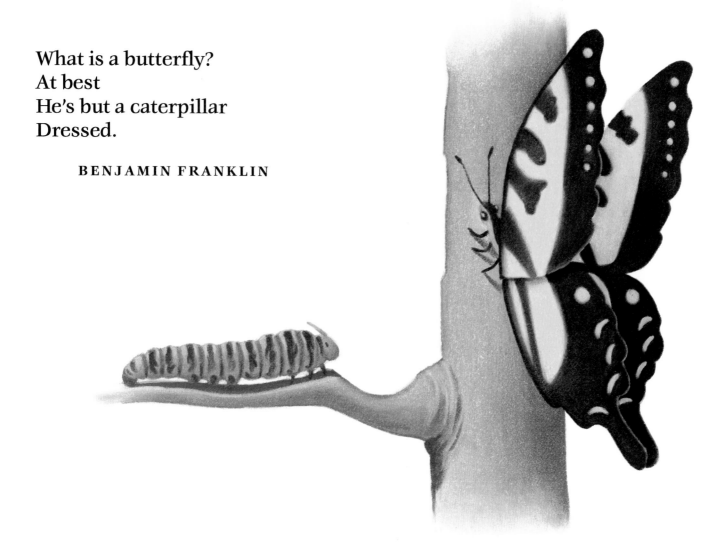

Bumblebee

I sat as still
as a playing-dead possum
and watched a bee
on a clover blossom,

Watched him poking
his long thin tongue
into the blossoms
pink and young,

Heard him bumble
and sort of sneeze
as pollen stuck
to his two hind knees.

I held my breath
as the bee buzzed over,
and hoped *I* didn't
look sweet as clover.

AILEEN FISHER

Ladybug

With spots
of black on red
she darted
through
my flower bed

then

quickly fled.

She
fluttered
from
a leaf.

Her visit
far
too brief.

I wanted
her
to
stay.

Today,
that
teeny-tiny,

sheeny-shiny,
ladybug
just
took
my
breath
away.

LEE BENNETT HOPKINS

Inch-Worm

Little green inch-worm,
Inch-worm, inch.
You can't hurt me,
You don't pinch.
Never did anyone
Any harm
So *take* your little green walk
Up my arm.

DOROTHY ALDIS

Hey, Bug!

Hey, bug, stay!
Don't run away.
I know a game that we can play.

I'll hold my fingers very still
and you can climb a finger-hill.

No, no.
Don't go.

Here's a wall—a tower, too,
a tiny bug town, just for you.
I've a cookie. You have some.
Take this oatmeal cookie crumb.

Hey, bug, stay!
Hey, bug!
Hey!

LILIAN MOORE

Bugs

I like bugs.
Black bugs,
Green bugs,
Bad bugs,
Mean bugs,
Any kind of bug,

A bug in a rug,
A bug in the grass,
A bug on the sidewalk,
A bug in a glass—
I like bugs.

Round bugs,
Shiny bugs,
Fat bugs,
Buggy bugs,
Big bugs,
Ladybugs,
I like bugs.

MARGARET WISE BROWN

Lee Bennett Hopkins is the author/anthologist of more than fifty books, many of them award or honor winners, including three novels. A graduate of Kean College, the Bank Street College of Education, and Hunter College, he received the University of Southern Mississippi Medallion in 1989 for "lasting contributions to children's literature."

Lee Bennett Hopkins lives in Scarborough, New York.

Peter Palagonia has illustrated two other books for children. He has also worked on theater posters, magazines, set designs, and murals. He lives in Sherman, Connecticut.

The illustrations for this book were done in colored pencil. The book is set in 16 Point ITC Veljovic. Typography by Lynn Braswell.